My World of Science

HEAVY
AND LIGHT

Angela Royston

Heinemann Library
Chicago, Illinois

© 2003 Heinemann Library
a division of Reed Elsevier Inc.
Chicago, Illinois

Customer Service 888-454-2279

Visit our website at www.heinemannlibrary.com

All rights reserved. No part of this publication may be reproduced or transmitted in any form or by any means, electronic or mechanical, including photocopying, recording, taping, or any information storage and retrieval system, without permission in writing from the publisher.

Designed by Jo Hinton-Malivoire and Tinstar Design Limited
Originated by Blenheim Colour, Ltd.
Printed and bound in China by South China Printing Company
Photo research by Maria Joannou and Sally Smith

07 06 05 04 03
10 9 8 7 6 5 4 3 2 1

Library of Congress Cataloging-in-Publication Data
Royston, Angela.
  Heavy and light / Angela Royston.
      p. cm. – (My world of science)
Summary: An introduction to the physical properties of weight and buoyancy, including everyday examples.
Includes bibliographical references (p.) and index.
  ISBN 1-40340-853-X (HC), 1-40343-166-3 (Pbk)
  1. Weight (Physics)–Juvenile literature. 2. Buoyant ascent (Hydrodynamics)–Juvenile literature. [1. Weight (Physics) 2. Floating bodies.] I. Title.
  QC106 .R69 2003
  530.8'1–dc21
                              2002009401

Acknowledgments
The author and publishers are grateful to the following for permission to reproduce copyright material:
pp. 4, 5, 6, 7, 8, 9, 10, 11, 12, 13, 14, 15, 16, 17, 18, 19, 25 Trevor Clifford; p. 20 PhotoDisc; pp. 21, 24 Corbis; p. 22 Collections; p. 23 Alamy Images; p. 26 H. Rogers/Trip; p. 27 Robert Harding Picture Library; p. 28 Fortean Picture Library; p. 29 Pictor International.

Cover photograph by Trevor Clifford.

Every effort has been made to contact copyright holders of any material reproduced in this book. Any omissions will be rectified in subsequent printings if notice is given to the publisher.

Some words are shown in bold, **like this.** You can find out what they mean by looking in the glossary.

Contents

Heavy and Light

Some things are heavy and some things are light. The television and the flowerpot are heavy. It is hard to lift heavy things.

All of these things are light. They are easy to lift. The cotton ball is the lightest thing here.

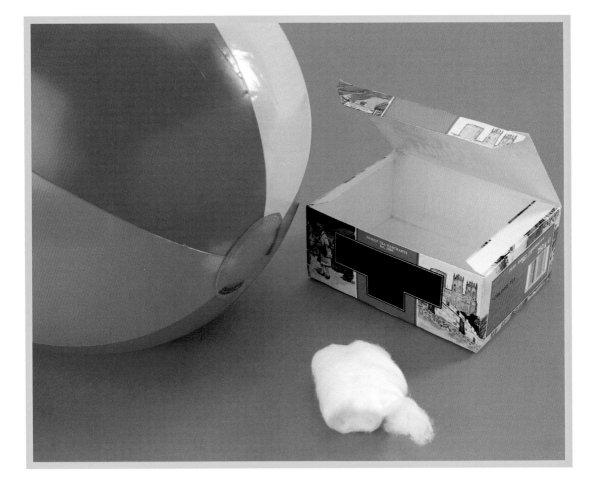

Comparing Weight

This girl is holding a book and a teddy bear. She can feel how heavy they are. The book is heavier than the teddy bear.

Weight means how heavy
something feels. Oranges and
apples are about the same weight.
It is hard to tell which is heavier.

Weighing

The girl wants to **weigh** the shovel. She puts it on one side of a **scale.** Then she adds weights to the other side.

She adds more weights to the scale until it becomes **level.** This means the weights are as heavy as the shovel.

Heavy Materials

Some **materials** are heavier than others. The feather and the pencil are about the same size. But the pencil is heavier. It is made of wood.

Big things are usually heavier than small things. The paper clip and the car are made of **steel.** But the car is much heavier than the paper clip.

Light Materials

Some metals are lighter than others. This stepladder is light. It is made of **aluminum**. An **iron** stepladder would be too heavy to lift.

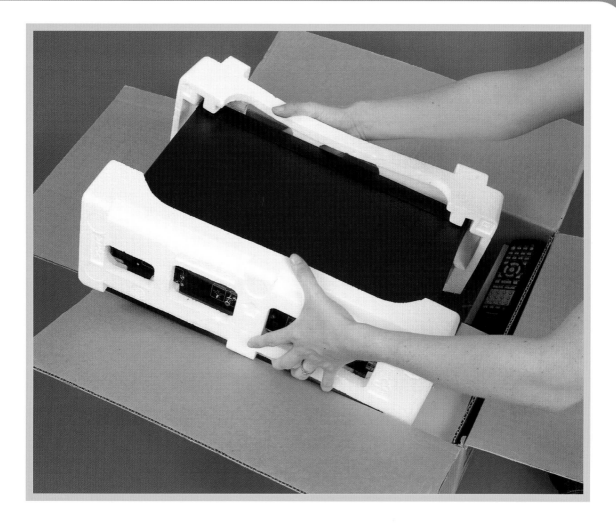

These white blocks are made from a kind of plastic. They protect the video recorder. But they are also light and easy to lift.

Water Can Be Heavy

This plastic **container** feels light when it is empty. But the container becomes heavy when it is filled with water.

Wool sweaters are usually light. But when they are washed, the wool soaks up a lot of water. The sweater gets very heavy.

Filled with Air

Balloons are light because they are
filled with air. You just have to tap
a balloon to keep it from falling.

These things are all light. They have air trapped inside them. If you squeeze them, they lose some of the air and become smaller.

Does It Float or Sink?

Things that float in water are light for their size. The rubber duck, the balloon, and the sponge are floating. They are filled with air.

These objects do not float. They are heavy for their size. Heavy things usually **sink** in water.

Heavy Things Can Float

Ships are large and heavy. They float because they are filled with air.
The air inside a ship makes it light.

This is the top part of a big ship. It hit some rocks and filled with water. This made the ship too heavy to float, and it **sank.**

Using Floats

People use **armbands** when they are learning to swim. Armbands are light because they are filled with air. They help people float in the water.

Lane dividers separate the different parts of this pool. The dividers have floats on them. The floats keep the dividers from **sinking.**

Anchors and Weights

Ships have heavy **anchors.** They **sink** to the bottom of the sea and dig into the sand or stones. This keeps a ship from floating away.

This **aquarium** plant has metal **weights** attached to it. The weight keeps the plant from floating around in the aquarium.

weight

Blowing in the Wind

The wind can move very light things.
These leaves are so light that the wind
moves them around easily.

Dandelion seeds are very light. They can float very far before they fall to the ground. New dandelion plants grow where the seeds land.

Lighter than Air

This is a **blimp.** It is filled with a gas called **helium.** Helium is much lighter than air, so the blimp floats.

These balloons are also filled with helium. Do not let go of a helium balloon. If you do, it will float higher and higher into the sky.

Glossary

aluminum very light metal
anchor piece of metal tied to the end of a rope or chain. The anchor keeps a boat from floating away.
aquarium tank filled with water where living animals and plants are kept
armband band of plastic that can be filled with air. It helps keep people afloat while swimming.
blimp aircraft filled with helium that floats in the air
container something that holds something else
dandelion common plant with a yellow flower and jagged leaves
helium gas that is lighter than air
iron very heavy metal
lane divider floating rope used to divide a pool
level at the same height as something else
material what a thing is made of
scale tool used to find out how much something weighs
sink move downward in water
steel kind of strong metal
weigh having a certain weight; or, measuring an object's weight
weight how heavy something is; or, object used to measure other objects
wool material for clothes made from the hair of sheep

More Books to Read

Madgwick, Wendy. *Super Materials.* Austin, Tex.: Raintree Publishers, 1999.

Riley, Peter. *Materials and Processes.* Danbury, Conn.: Scholastic Library Publishing, 1999.

Willis, Shirley. *Tell Me How Ships Float.* Danbury, Conn.: Scholastic Library Publishing, 2000.

Index